THE SUN IS GOING DOWN FOR ALL OF US.

THE SUN IS GOING DOWN FOR ALL OF US.

Notes on the Murder of Mother Earth

Compiled & Edited by
JANE WILKIE

STANYAN BOOKS

RANDOM HOUSE

ACKNOWLEDGMENTS

Sincere thanks are extended
to the following for permis-
sion to include material
in this work:
Don Widener, producer of
KNBC's *Timetable For
Disaster* and *Slow Guillotine*.
The Victor Gruen Founda-
tion For Environmental
Planning. The Los Angeles
Times. The Washington Post.
The New York Times.
Look Magazine for lines from
an article by Elizabeth
Alston. McCall's Magazine
for material from an article
by Professor Paul R. Ehrlich.
Newsweek.

A Stanyan book
Published by Stanyan Books,
8721 Sunset Blvd., Suite C
Hollywood, California 90069,
and by Random House, Inc.
201 East 50th Street,
New York, N.Y. 10022

Library of Congress Catalog
Card Number: 9-149508

Printed in U.S.A.
Designed by Hy Fujita

For My Sister

Who in April of 1970 said she thought "all this
ecology stuff is only a fad, the latest ploy
for politicians."

A word on the photographs illustrating this book.
Other than our planet, contributed by NASA, the
pictures herein were taken over the past two years
by Lenstour Photos. Some of our world still looks
this way—but less and less every day. Therefore,
the shot of the now dead crane flying across the
sun on page 24 is little more than a documentary.

— Jane Wilkie

Listen and hear
the sound of the dying grass bleed.
It's bleeding for man,
and the fool,
he just won't understand.

— *Rod McKuen — The Wind of Change*

"This planet is no longer that
which I have known and loved ...
I know the world must change.
I am not revolted. I am simply
noting that there are no longer
any nightingales in my garden.
I am incapable of existing in a
universe which has destroyed nature."

> — *Francois Mauriac*
> *(written shortly before his*
> *death in September, 1970)*

The Way It Is

Visible air pollution has been spotted over
the North Pole.

Every three days, population growth equals the
number of men killed (600,000) in *all* the wars
fought by the United States.

The air over the Atlantic Ocean is twice as dirty
as it was at the turn of the century.

The United States dumps 48.2 million tons of
solid waste into the Atlantic Ocean each year.

Smog has been found in medical oxygen.

On this planet, perhaps as many as 20 million people, *mostly children,* starve to death each year. Of the 3.6 billion population on earth, between one and two billion are hungry or malnourished.

Even though Americans represent only 6% of the earth's total population, this country uses more than 40% of the world's scarce resources.

A pathologist at the University of Southern California school of medicine believes that all people over 12 years of age— *whether they live in a city or the country—* have damaged lungs.

The Parthenon, symbol of the glory of ancient Greece, is beginning to crumble. Its ruins have stood for 2500 years — but it cannot resist the damage of smog.

Boston lives under an umbrella of dirt particles that is not dispersed by either rain or wind.

Federal health officials have admitted that poisons such as lead, mercury and arsenic have been found in dangerous amounts in beef, shellfish and chicken livers.

4800 pounds of lead daily are being dumped into the lower Mississippi River.

In western Nevada and the Lake Tahoe basin, forest fire lookout stations are being phased out because of low visibility due to smog.

Every major stream in Europe is contaminated.

The Air

Automobiles cause an estimated 60% of all air pollution in the United States. Experimenting with assorted fuels, mufflers and engines, Detroit has yet to come up with a car that will give us clean air.

In the mountains 8000 feet above the city of San Bernardino, California, a thousand acres of Ponderosa pine have been logged because they were dying of smog.

A doctor specializing in respiratory diseases urges urban citizens to get extra sleep during periods of heavy smog. They should also avoid stimulating foods and drinks.

In the past ten years, the amount of junk in the air over the Hawaiian Islands has increased 35%.

According to Ralph Nader, there are two sources of vehicle pollution that haven't yet even been studied . . . the matter that enters our lungs and bodies from both the grinding of rubber tires, and the asbestos from the grinding and wearing of brake linings.

Due in great part to smog, the temperature of our
planet has risen a half-degree in recent years.
This doesn't sound particularly sinister, but
British scientists have affirmed that polar masses
are already beginning to melt. If the situation
continues, millions of people will lose their
lives in a great flood.

If the Middle Ages had exploited the earth's surface as we are doing, we probably wouldn't be on it now.

— *Jacob Burckhardt*

The Water

Water is the only drink which absolutely quenches thirst ... Most of the other liquors ... are but palliatives.

> — *Brillat-Savarin*
> *1825*

Millions of Americans are drinking water that is potentially hazardous due to contamination. Samples have been found to contain fecal bacteria, lead, copper, iron, manganese, nitrate. A few even exceeded the chromium and arsenic limits.

Among plant operators of the country's public water systems surveyed, 76% were found to be inadequately trained in fundamental water microbiology.

Lake Mead has algae buildups; phosphates and nitrates pour into it every day. If the situation is not corrected, Lake Mead will become a dead body of water.

Back in 1899, the Refuse Act became law in the United States. It prohibited the dumping of wastes into American waters, under penalty of fine. It was only in December of 1970 that the President enforced the law by requiring industry to obtain a federal permit for any such dumping.

Young citizens of a southern city formed a commando group late in 1970, broke into the local sewage plant and dumped yellow dye into untreated sewage. The following day, faucets in the city spewed yellow water—and people in at least one American town learned what they had been drinking.

According to Webster, water is odorless and tasteless. This might well rouse laughter among residents of certain areas whose faucets dispense a liquid that's foamy (from detergent residual), murky (from algae), swimming-pool smelling (from germ-killing chlorine). A recent Federal survey reports that 30% of U.S. tap water is tainted.

The Earth

Man bulldozes the trees, slices the mountains,
and covers the land with buildings and parking
lots. We are smothering the earth with concrete.

As a people Americans are the biggest single contributor of dangerous pollutants to the land, water, and atmosphere. We are the prime destroyers of ecological systems, that complex web of relationships among living things and their physical surroundings. All human life on our little spaceship depends on those systems; they supply *all* our food, *all* our oxygen, and ultimately dispose of our wastes.

The earth is sprayed with poisons to kill pests, and blanketed with contamination from industrial waste. Our Forestry Service sprays brush and weeds with herbicides that are the same defoliant chemicals used in Vietnam. And the spray drifts into inhabited areas.

The last unprotected stand of Torrey pines, the ice-age trees on the southern coast of California, will be bulldozed by land developers. A citizens' drive for $900,000 to save the trees fell short of its goal.

The toilets of the nation's railroads are a serious health hazard, dumping millions of pounds of untreated, germ-carrying human wastes on our environment. Yet the president of the Association of American railroads denied that a health problem exists.

It will take a 'revolution in values' to save the world. What is needed is a new ethic that thinks and acts in terms of guardianship of the planet and its life.

— *Mrs. Charles A. Lindbergh*

The Sea

The oceans are in danger of dying. People do not
realize that all pollution ends up in the seas.
The earth is less polluted. It is washed by rain
which carries everything into the oceans, where
life has diminished by 40% in 20 years . . .
In the past, the sea renewed itself; it was a
continuous cycle. But this cycle is being upset.

— *Jacques Cousteau*

Thor Heyerdahl, reporting on his voyage across
the Pacific in a papyrus boat, said that he saw
garbage and waste in the middle of the sea. "Not
just a spot here and there, but miles and miles of it."

Prof. John Isaacs, director of marine life research
for Scripps Institute of Oceanography at San
Diego, said dumping toxic gas into the sea water
could produce "a charnel house of dead creatures."
There is far more life in the deep sea than many
people expect, according to recent studies,
Isaacs said. And animals, he added, are attracted
by dead animals.
"It is quite possible," he said, "that this could
lead to a perpetual trap, with animal going
after animal."

A 21-mile-square patch of polluted water—dubbed the "Dead Sea" because of damage to marine life—is spreading toward New York and New Jersey shores at the rate of a mile a year.

Population:

Any American woman who has more than two children is committing all of her children to an early death.

To those who argue that America's population is considerably less than that in the crowded areas of the world, the fact is that a child in a middle-class American family will use 50 times more power than will any citizen of India. He will consume more gas, electricity, food— all of which create waste.

Population growth is the root cause of pollution. The more people, the more waste—garbage, sewage, trash, and the stuff that spews from industrial chimneys.

By the year 2000 A.D., the earth's population will be twice what it is today. Today's population growth has been described as equal to "the arrival of 20 divisions from outer space daily, without K rations."

Food:

Dangerous amounts of DDT have been found in lettuce, salmon, turkey and mackerel.

Fish caught in waters off the American coasts have been found cancerous. The species with malignant tumors or lesions are sole, halibut, spotted turbot, white croakers, and sea bass.

In March 1968, Sweden received a warning from its health officials: Do not eat fish from most fresh or coastal waters more than once a week.

The United States has been unbelievably tardy in recognizing the danger of mercury.
Said Victor Lambou, Federal Water Quality biologist, "I don't think you can find any chemical that is potentially worse for man."

— Victor Cohn
Washington Post

California biologists are trying to determine the cause of the destruction of thousands of striped bass and sturgeon along a 15-mile stretch of the Carquinez Straits near Vallejo. A biologist for the State Water Resources Board said the fish kill may be related to waste discharge from plants and oil refineries near the straits—which connect the Sacramento River and San Francisco Bay.

Mercury is widely used to treat seed grain in order to prevent fungus infection . . . and the fodder is fed to farm animals. Such wheat fed to pigs gravely crippled three New Mexico farm children last winter.

Several brands of candy bars have been withdrawn from the market because they were found to contain rodent hairs.

What's it like to watch pollution kill a horse?

Ask Janet Wesner:

"We threw some hay to the horses. They were up on top of the hill, and they ran down to the hay and began eating.

"After about five minutes of eating hay, the horses began to cough. And after about another five minutes, they began stretching their necks. You could see they were needing air.

"One young mare—she was 6 years old—just rolled over . . . She was rolling, just anything to try to get air. She was, you could tell, suffocating to death. And it was about a half an hour from the time that the first symptoms set in to the time she was dead."

For the past nine years, Bingo and Janet Wesner have been raising horses in the rolling brown hills of Solano County near Benicia, 35 miles northeast of San Francisco.

... Dr. Fred Ottoboni of the State Department of Public Health has diagnosed the specific cause of the deaths as lead poisoning and, in a written report, said the source "appears to be pasture grass which is contaminated with lead."

... The most likely source of lead emission has long been fixed as the American Smelting and Refining Co. at Selby, across the strait.

... The plant belches 109 pounds of lead daily out of its giant smokestack, plus 129 pounds of other metals and 63 tons of sulfur dioxide.

— *William Endicott*
L.A. Times 7/14/70

🦋 🦋 🦋

POISONS
Yes, poisons!

Mercury poisoning, like DDT, can be deadly, affecting brain and nerve cells. It tends to be cumulative in both man and nature.

All this stuff like DDT, PCB, mercury, cadmium, went into the water, into agriculture, into our food, and now come into our bodies via the food and the air ... It is a matter of life and death of this civilization.

> — *Professor Hans Palmstierna,*
> *Secretary to the Swedish*
> *Advisory Committee*

City dwellers already have in their bodies 100 times the amount of lead that would be present under normal conditions. Add a light amount to this, and acute lead poisoning could result.

When Rachel Carson wrote *Silent Spring* ten years ago, exposing the dangers of DDT, she was attacked by both industry and science. Once hailed as a boon to humanity, DDT is now known to be a dread pollutant that is carried in rains and ocean currents.

In Moscow, where gasoline is lead-free, the concentration of lead in the soil is 19 parts per million. In Los Angeles, the concentration is 3000 parts per million.

The bottom of the Baltic Sea is carpeted with lethal junk piles, including most of the 62,000 tons of chemical weapons produced by the Nazi Reich and captured by the Allies. Like their American counterparts today, British and Russian officers thought it best to dump the stockpile at sea . . . "The containers pose a danger to our population," warns Danish Fisheries Minister Anders Normann. "We don't know how the gases will behave after corrosion has destroyed the containers and the gas begins to move freely."

Condensed from Newsweek
Copyright Newsweek, Inc. 8/24/70

"We have met the enemy, and he is us."

— Pogo

THE MILITARY...

How it Contributes
its Share to Pestilence
and Pollution

In 1966 the Army stored 200 shells filled with
nerve gas (reportedly the deadly VX, a drop of
which on the skin will kill a human being) on a
frozen Alaskan lake. The lethal stockpile was
then forgotten; with the spring thaw, the shells
sank to the bottom of the lake. Until 1969, when
a new commanding officer ordered the lake
drained and the shells recovered, the Army had
neglected to order the gas destroyed
by chemicals.

Little is known outside the Pentagon about what the miltary has dumped into the sea in the past. The House oceanography subcommittee has asked the army for a list, but as of August, 1970 had not received it.

WASHINGTON, July 29—The Army will move two trainloads of small rockets filled with the lethal nerve gas GB through the South to be dumped into the Atlantic Ocean, Representative Cornelius Gallagher said today.

418 concrete and steel blocks each containing 30 M-55 rockets will be loaded aboard a hulk at the naval weapons plant at Charleston, S. C., and towed about 250 miles off the coast to be sunk in 1,500 feet of water. According to a United Nations report, less than one drop of GB can paralyze and kill a victim within minutes of contact by damaging his nervous system.

Dr. Howard L. Sanders, a senior scientist at the Woods Hole Oceanographic Institute at Woods Hole, Mass., said the Army's handling of nerve gas and its plan to dump it in the Atlantic Ocean off Florida was "sheer, unbelievable inefficiency and stupidity" that could have a "profound effect on the environment."

QUESTION: If the disposal of "outmoded" nerve gas caused such a flap in 1970, is the Pentagon thinking about how to get rid of the gases created today when *they* become outmoded?

Army Unsure If Gas Coffins Will Break

An attorney for the Army conceded that officials did not know whether nerve gas coffins would break apart from the pressure when sunk in three-mile deep waters of the Atlantic ... The Army said that one of the coffins contains deadlier gas than the others but confessed it had lost track of which one it was.

— Los Angeles Times 8/70

Navy Can't Determine If Nerve Gas Escaped

Aboard the USS Hartley—(UPI) The Navy abandoned its efforts Wednesday to determine whether a sinking Liberty ship released its cargo of deadly poison gas into the Atlantic Ocean 282 miles off the Florida coast ... The Navy said its special equipment failed to find any trace of the ship.

Sewage:

You are what you eat . . . again and again and again.

"About one-third of the nation's population is not
served by a sewer system at all . . . In addition to
these (67 million) there are 10 million people who
do have sewers but discharge their wastes without
treatment . . . The waste loads from municipal
systems are expected to quadruple over the
next 50 years."

> — *Report from the Council on
> Environmental Quality, 8/70*

Monterey Bay, famed as one of the west coast's
most beautiful areas, is so polluted that marine
biology students get typhoid and hepatitis shots
before skin-diving. Towns surrounding the bay feed
partly treated sewage into the ocean — and socially
elite Pebble Beach pipes its human wastes
into the bay — raw.

All sewage discharged into the Hudson River from
Manhattan is raw. There is no treatment of it
whatsoever . . . Up to now, people thought rivers
were built to carry away man's waste.

Rep. Richard McCarthy (D-N.Y.) jumped into the Hudson River and surfaced after seven minutes. "I'd have stayed down longer but I didn't want to get infected. It's worse than I thought — I couldn't even see the bottom."

People still fish by the sewer outlet in the Hudson River. One angler said, "It's not too bad, but I don't like the stuff I have to pick off my line."

It is very difficult to persuade people that,
if you can't actually see the pollution,
it's doing any harm.

> — *Dr. Robert Clark, University*
> *of Newcastle-on-Tyne, England*

What's Left of Our Wildlife...

So that we might wear fur coats (in Florida, California?), we kill whales to feed commercially grown minks. And on ice floes off Alaska, hunters skin live baby seals and leave them to die in agony.

90% of the vicuna in Peru have been killed in the past ten years—to end up on our backs.

The red wolf and the Florida panther are becoming extinct through loss of habitat.

The cormorant, the grebe, the pelican are all in trouble. The pelican used to breed half way up the Western coast; now they are seen only off the Mexican coast.

Famed for its beauty, the tiger of India now numbers less than 3000.

The birds are dying. Sea birds are laying eggs with shells so thin that many of the young do not survive. Those that do often cannot learn to fly.

The wild horses of our west have been virtually wiped out, killed for pet food.

Also vanishing . . . the snow leopard, the kangaroo, the giant green sea turtle—the latter killed to obtain oil for skin creams.

Oil slicks off the coast of Santa Barbara in California have killed untold thousands of birds, sea otters and seals.

Through the use of pesticides, America is killing off her own national symbol, the bald eagle.

During the winter of 1968-1969, thousands of dead birds were found in the Irish Sea. A toxic industrial chemical called PCB was discovered in their tissues.

🐿 🐿 🐿

Among the creatures disappearing from the earth ... the sea otter, antelope, panda, crested ibis, Asian lion, sandhill crane, Bachman's warbler, ivory-billed woodpecker, Indian rhinoceros, whooping crane, Atlantic sturgeon, tule elk, bowhead whale.

Some of us say, "Who cares? Who needs a tule elk or a whooping crane?" Perhaps we don't *need* them today, but who knows what will be important to our descendants? If we live long enough to have any.

🐿 🐿 🐿

KILL COUNT IN CALIFORNIA ... In the past five years, over two million fish, birds and animals have been killed by pollution or pesticides. This figure does not include creatures that died due to the oil spill near Santa Barbara.

🐿 🐿 🐿

These wildlife deaths should remind us of the old miner's canary—a warning that something is terribly wrong with our environment.

If the birds and the animals are dying unnatural
deaths, so, one day, shall we.

Some Opinions...

The former head of the Los Angeles Air Pollution Control, who has spoken with scientists all over the world, believes that we have no more than 50 years left. "I think we will be lucky if we have 25."

Says Ralph Nader, "I think that is being generous."

Pollution recognizes no boundary, political or geographic. All men must share the guilt and the misery of pollution. In this sense, at least, we are one.

> — *Jack Lemmon, KNBC's* Timetable For Disaster

"Our intellectual life consists of a series of seven-day wonders, then we're off to something more exciting.

"The present indignation about the environment blew up very rapidly, like a squall of wind, and will probably die down with equal speed, like most American social criticism—mea culpa, mea culpa, mea maxima culpa, and then everything is taken care of."

> — *John Wilkinson, translator at the Center for the Study of Democratic Institutions*

All living things are our brothers.

> — *Sir Kenneth Clark*

So...

The majority of scientists think that man has both the time and intelligence to clean up the earth and its atmosphere. However, when several were asked on NBC's *Timetable For Disaster* if they think we *will* do it, they held little hope.

Sample answers:

I'm sorry. I am a pessimist in this regard. I feel that mankind will react only when it's too late and catastrophe is upon us.

> — *Dr. Clare Patterson, Professor of Geochemistry at Cal-Tech.*

I believe my child has a shorter life expectancy than I do.

> — *Dr. James Deacon, Professor of Biology at University of Nevada*

If we keep on as we've been going in the last generation, we're headed for disaster.

> — *Dr. Donald Abbott, Assistant Director of Hopkins Marine Station, Pacific Grove, Calif.*

I'm 27 years old, and I think I'll live to see the end.

> — *President, North American Habitat Preservation Society*

IT'S *YOUR* PLANET – WHAT
ARE YOU GOING TO DO ABOUT IT?

We'll never know if boycotting enemies of the earth is effective—until we try. A start:

Do not buy the following . . .

1. No-deposit, no-return containers or non-recyclable cans.
2. Detergents with NTA or phosphate content. See page 60.
3. Colored tissues, napkins, toilet paper, etc. Dyes pollute waterways.
4. Pesticides containing DDT, Dieldrin, Lindane, Chlordane, Heptachlor, Endrin, Aldrin, 2, 4, 5-T, BHD, Taxaphene—or any compound containing lead, mercury, or arsenic.
5. Foil wrapping. It cannot be re-processed and used again.
6. Disposable diapers, or items with packaging that is merely decorative. These increase demands for paper, and thus timber.
7. Fur coats, feathers, anything from wild species.
8. Recreation devices using motors—dune buggies, power boats, snowmobiles, etc.

At the first International Conference of Ocean Pollution Experts, held in Rome, American representatives said that funds are inadequate for agencies recently organized to control environment in our country.

🌹 🌹 🌹

We need $30 billion dollars for air pollution; $60 billion for water pollution, and $10 billion dollars for proper sewage treatment plants. The present administration is fighting for 1.4 million dollars. We can't possibly do the job.

> — *Doyle Grabarck, President*
> *North American Habitat*
> *Preservation Society*

🌹 🌹 🌹

WRITE : The President, your Senator, your Congressman, your Mayor and City Council.

(Say something nice about them in the first paragraph. These are the letters they usually read first.)

DO's and DON'Ts in Daily Life

DO!

1. Make a compost heap instead of burning leaves. (Paper can be composted).
2. If possible, use a car pool for commuting.
3. Carry a litter bag and collect other people's trash as well as your own. (Try for a high score of beer cans on any highway.)
4. Keep your garbage and trash containers tightly closed.
5. Keep all machines in good working order, particularly your car.
6. Take your own shopping bag to market. Leave unnecessary packaging with the store manager, or, to really give him the message, mail him all excess packaging with an explanatory letter.
7. Save old newspapers for paper drives. A phone call to the Boy Scouts will bring a pickup.
8. Save all bottles and cans. The Scouts can also give you the location of the nearest re-cycling agency.
9. Limit your family to two children. If you want more, adopt.
10. Order your Christmas tree from a nursery. Pick out a tree that can be potted, and later planted or given back to the nursery.

DON'T!

1. Don't let your car engine idle needlessly.
2. Don't drive when you can walk or use public transportation . . . or a bicycle.
3. Don't allow water to run unnecessarily.
4. Don't allow barbecue fires to smoke excessively. And don't burn paper plates, etc. after the meal.
5. Don't use a chemical spray or insect strip. The old-fashioned fly swatter is still the best bug-killer.

As an example of apathy (or ignorance), the following result of a poll taken by Congressman Barry Goldwater Jr. is typical. His constituents voted in 1970 on the relative importance of national issues—in this manner. 1. Vietnam; 2. Crime; 3. Cost of living; 4. **Environment**; 5. Communism; 6. Education.

🌹🌹🌹

WRITE: The President, your Senator, your Congressman, your Mayor and City Council.

Maybe their mail is light this week and your letter will get through.

🌹🌹🌹

If we're going to avert a disaster we're going to have to make the same kind of a commitment that we've made to the construction of weapons systems and to the exploration of space.

— *Sen. Gaylord Nelson (D., Wisc.)*

🌹🌹🌹

The famous smog of Los Angeles is caused mainly by automobiles. The city has the cleanest industrial basin in the world—an achievement following 40,000 criminal suits, 90% of which were won by the city. This lesson doesn't seem to get through to other big cities.

I think there is an unawareness on the part of officials nationwide of just what the seriousness of our problem really is. I don't think they understand; but they better understand it soon.

If they haven't got the guts to do it, then they better get out of the way and let somebody get in who can do the job, because it's got to be done.

— *Louis Fuller, Former APCD Officer*

WRITE: The President, your Senator, your Congressman, your Mayor and City Council.

If your letters still aren't being answered, isn't it time we got a President, senator, congressman, mayor, or city council who *will* answer? Remember, all of us are responsible for the destruction we are bringing upon ourselves.

Detergent is a Dirty Word*

Phosphates are added to detergents to help disperse dirt particles. But phosphates nourish algae, which grow in our water until these organisms cut off both light and oxygen to fish and all waterlife.

In an effort to cooperate, some (not all) soap manufacturers replaced phosphate with NTA—nitrilo triacetic acid—and then advertised that their detergents contained no phosphate. Leading chemists, however, have found that NTA is perhaps more dangerous than phosphate, because it transports toxic ions and causes birth defects.

Where does that leave us? Back with old-fashioned soap and, if you're lucky enough to have it, soft water. All detergent residue can be removed from clothes by washing them in hot water and four tablespoons of Arm and Hammer washing soda. Subsequently, each laundry should be done with the proper amount of soap and three tablespoons of washing soda.

*But Not For Long

As we go to press, Sears is bringing out a new detergent with neither NTA nor phosphates—called Sears Laundry Detergent—and manufacturers will undoubtedly be coming up with similar products. Watch for them—ecology begins at home.

**Tomorrow is too late!
Even today is in doubt**

If you are
concerned with ecology,
send $1.00 to:

ROD McKUEN FOUNDATION
BOX 2783
HOLLYWOOD, CALIFORNIA
90028

for the above decal. All profits from
the sale of the decal will be applied
toward scholarships for students
studying Animal Husbandry and research grants for the further study
of our ecological environment.